Vorwort

Liebe Schülerin, lieber Schüler,

in *Grammar and phrases* findest du die gesamte Grammatik und alle *Useful phrases* aus Green Line 3 und 4 übersichtlich zusammengefasst.

Aus Green Line 3 und 4 kennst du bereits den Grammatikanhang, der alle Grammatikthemen der Units enthält. Dieser Teil hat dir bestimmt schon oft geholfen, wenn du ein Thema noch einmal nachschlagen wolltest, das du nicht richtig verstanden hast, deine Hausaufgaben gemacht hast oder dich auf einen Test oder eine Klassenarbeit vorbereiten wolltest.

Im **Grammar**-Teil von *Grammar and phrases* sind alle grammatischen Inhalte der letzten beiden Jahre nach den wichtigsten Themen geordnet. So kannst du jederzeit ganz leicht alle Grammatikthemen nachschlagen, die du bis jetzt im Unterricht gelernt hast.

Nach dem **Grammar**-Teil folgt der **Phrases**-Teil. Sicher haben dir die *Useful phrases*, denen du immer wieder in Green Line begegnest, schon oft dabei geholfen, dich bei Unterhaltungen oder im Unterricht richtig auszudrücken und in Alltagssituationen die richtigen Worte parat zu haben. In diesem Teil sind alle *Useful phrases* aus Green Line 3 und 4 unter verschiedenen Themen zusammengefasst. So kannst du für jede Situation die richtigen Worte ganz einfach nachschlagen.

Ganz am Ende des Hefts findest du eine Liste von nützlichen *Classroom phrases* zum Nachschlagen und die Liste der unregelmäßigen Verben, in der du nachsehen kannst, wenn dir eine Verbform mal nicht einfällt.

Weiterhin viel Spaß und Erfolg beim Lernen mit *Green Line!*

Inhalt

1	Vorwort
2	Grammar
34	Useful phrases
45	In the classroom
47	Irregular verbs

Legende

SB 3, Unit 1: Unit im Schülerbuch, in der das Grammatikthema vorkommt.
SB 4, 53: Seite im Schülerbuch, auf der du die *Useful phrases* finden kannst.

Grammar — Inhalt

Damit du dich im Englischen mündlich und schriftlich gut ausdrücken kannst, ist es wichtig, die grammatischen Regeln der Sprache richtig zu verwenden. Auf den nächsten Seiten findest du die wichtigsten Grammatikthemen aus Green Line 3 und 4 thematisch zusammengefasst. Diese Zusammenfassung kann dir helfen, wenn du deine Hausaufgaben machst, wenn du dich auf einen Test oder eine Arbeit vorbereiten möchtest oder wenn du einfach etwas nachschlagen oder wiederholen möchtest, das du nicht ganz verstanden hast.

Inhalt

Pronomen
4	1	Reflexivpronomen

Die Zeitformen des Verbs
6	2	Das Futur mit *will*
8	3	Die Verlaufsform der Vergangenheit
9	4	Die Verlaufsform des Perfekts
12	5	Das Plusquamperfekt
13	6	Die Verlaufsform des Plusquamperfekts

Das Gerundium und der Infinitiv
15	7	Das Gerundium
17	8	Der Infinitiv mit und ohne *to*
20	9	Das *gerund* oder der Infinitiv mit *to:* Bedeutungsunterschiede

Das Passiv
21	10	Das Passiv

Inhalt **Grammar** G

Direkte und indirekte Rede

23	11	Aussagen in der indirekten Rede
25	12	Zeit- und Ortsangaben in der indirekten Rede
26	13	Fragen in der indirekten Rede
27	14	Befehle, Aufforderungen und Bitten in der indirekten Rede

Satz und Satzgefüge

28	15	Notwendige und nicht-notwendige Relativsätze
30	16	Bedingungssätze Typ 1
31	17	Bedingungssätze Typ 2
33	18	Bedingungssätze Typ 3

G Grammar — Pronomen

Pronomen

1 **You have to push yourself.** → SB 3, Unit 2

Reflexivpronomen
Reflexive pronouns and each other

Wow! Olivia plays the sax really well. Did **you** teach **her**?

No, I didn't. **She** taught **herself**. And **she** even wrote the music **herself**.

> *Im Englischen verwendest du die Reflexivpronomen (Pronomen auf -self / -selves), wenn das **Objekt** sich auf das **Subjekt** im Satz zurückbezieht. Subjekt und Objekt sind dabei **dieselbe Person**.*
> *Du verwendest die Reflexivpronomen auch, wenn du eine Person oder Sache im Satz hervorheben willst.*

- *Die Singularformen der Reflexivpronomen enden auf* -self (herself); *die Pluralformen auf* -selves (themselves).

	1. Person	**2. Person**	**3. Person**
Singular:	(I) … mysel**f**	(you) … yoursel**f**	(he, she, it) … himsel**f**, hersel**f**, itsel**f**
Plural:	(we) … oursel**ves**	(you) … yoursel**ves**	(they) … themsel**ves**

- *Die -self-Pronomen kommen im Englischen als Reflexivpronomen (rückbezügliche Pronomen) und als verstärkende Pronomen vor.*

Pronomen **Grammar** G

a) Reflexiver Gebrauch

○ Im Englischen verwendest du die Pronomen auf -self / -selves, wenn das **Objekt dieselbe Person** bezeichnet wie das **Subjekt**. In diesem Fall entsprechen sie den deutschen Pronomen mich / mir, dich / dir, sich (selbst), usw. Vergleiche:

Did **you** teach **her**?   her = andere Person (Objektpronomen)
She taught **herself**.   herself = dieselbe Person (Reflexivpronomen)

	Subjekt	Verb	Objekt / Reflexivpronomen	Deutsch
I'm so angry	I	could hit	myself.	ich – mich
Did	you	hurt	yourself?	du – dich / du – dir
Jay wants to become a famous singer.	He	really pushes	himself with singing and dancing.	er – sich
Claire often feels like	she's	talking to	herself.	sie – (mit) sich (selbst)
	We	always enjoy	ourselves.	wir – uns
Why can't	you	behave	yourselves?	ihr – euch
Don't worry about the boys.	They	can look after	themselves.	sie – sich

❗ Die Reflexivpronomen werden im Englischen wesentlich seltener gebraucht als im Deutschen. Viele Verben, die **im Deutschen reflexiv** sind, werden **im Englischen ohne -self** oder **-selves** gebildet.
How do you feel today? – Wie fühlst du **dich** heute?
I'm looking forward to the weekend. – Ich freue **mich** auf das Wochenende.

change	sich (ver)ändern	look forward to	sich freuen auf
decide	sich entscheiden	meet	sich treffen
feel	sich fühlen	relax	sich entspannen
hide	sich verstecken	remember	sich erinnern
hurry	sich beeilen	sit down	sich hinsetzen
imagine	sich vorstellen	worry	sich Sorgen machen

b) Verstärkender Gebrauch

○ Mit den Reflexivpronomen kannst du auch eine Person oder eine Sache im Satz besonders hervorheben. In diesem Fall entspricht myself, yourself, himself … dem deutschen **selbst / allein**:
Wow, that's a cool song. – Thanks, **I** wrote it **myself**. (selbst)
You don't have to help us. **We** can do it **ourselves**. (allein, ohne fremde Hilfe)

Grammar — Die Zeitformen des Verbs

c) Themselves *oder* each other?

- *Wenn du ausdrücken möchtest, dass zwischen Personen etwas wechselseitig geschieht oder es um Gegenseitigkeit geht, verwendest du* **each other**. *Im Deutschen wird* each other *meist mit* **sich**, **einander** *oder* **gegenseitig** *wiedergegeben.*

They're looking at **themselves**.

They're looking at **each other**.

❗ *Achte darauf, dass du die Reflexivpronomen nicht mit* each other *verwechselst.*

English summary

- The singular forms of the reflexive pronouns end in -**self** (myself); the plural forms end in -**selves** (ourselves).
- You use the reflexive pronoun
  a) when subject and object of the sentence are the same person: *He hurt himself.*
  b) as an emphasizing (*hervorhebendes*) pronoun: *Nobody helped me. I did it myself.*
- You use **each other** to talk about an interaction between people: *We talk to each other every day.*

Die Zeitformen des Verbs

2 I'll miss you so much!
Das Futur mit will
Will future

SB 3, Unit 1

But the house looks fantastic! I'm sure your mum **will be** happy there with all the farm animals to work with.

I**'ll miss** you so much!

Du verwendest das Futur mit will *für spontane Entscheidungen, Versprechen, Hoffnungen und Vorhersagen, die die Zukunft betreffen.*

Die Zeitformen des Verbs **Grammar** G

- *Mit dem* will future …
  a) *drückst du spontane Entscheidungen oder Versprechen aus.*

I**'ll text** you.
Holly and I **will visit** you in Cornwall.

  b) *machst du Vorhersagen über zukünftige Ereignisse.*
  (Der Sprecher kann diese nicht beeinflussen.)

Gwen:	We**'ll miss** you, Dave.
Assistant:	The trip to St Agnes **will take** about seven hours.

  c) *sagst du, was jemand über ein zukünftiges Ereignis denkt, hofft oder vermutet. Diese Sätze beginnen häufig mit* I hope, I think *oder* I'm sure.

Jay:	I think you**'ll make** lots of new friends quickly.
Dave:	I'm sure Sid **will hate** his new home.

- *Das* will future *bildest du für alle Personen aus dem Hilfsverb* **will (not) + Grundform des Verbs.** *Die Kurzform lautet* 'll *bzw. bei verneinten Sätzen* won't.

Aussage:	Dave hopes that his friends **will visit** him in St Agnes.
Verneinung:	Aunt Frances **won't come** to Cornwall with them.
Ergänzungsfrage:	What do you think Dave's new school **will be** like?
Entscheidungsfrage mit Kurzantwort:	**Will** your dad **find** work there? – Yes, he **will**. / No, he **won't**.

❗ *Um die Zukunftsform der Modalverben zu bilden, brauchst du ihre Ersatzformen:*

can, can't → (not) be able to:	Dave hopes his friends **will be able to** find enough money to visit him in St Agnes. … werden in der Lage sein …
can, can't, may, mustn't → (not) be allowed to:	The friends **won't be allowed to** go to Cornwall without an adult. … werden nicht … dürfen
must, needn't → (not) have to:	Holly **will have to** ask her mum for money. … wird … müssen

G Grammar — Die Zeitformen des Verbs

❗ *Mit dem* going-to *und dem* will future *kennst du zwei Zeitformen der Zukunft. Möchtest du über Zukünftiges sprechen, musst du abwägen:*
Für feststehende **Pläne** *oder* **Absichten** → going-to future:
The Prestons **are going to move** to Cornwall in summer.
Für **spontane Entscheidungen** → will future:
"I need to put all my things into boxes." – "Don't worry. I**'ll help** you."
Für **Vermutungen, Hoffnungen** *oder* **Vorhersagen** → will future:
I think Dave **will be** OK in Cornwall.

❗ *Verwechsle nicht „Ich will …" (= I want to …) und "I will …" (= Ich werde …).*

3 What were they doing when Holly took the picture? → SB 3, Unit 3

Die Verlaufsform der Vergangenheit
The past progressive

Look at this picture. Isn't it funny? I took it while we **were walking** around Glasgow.

Oh and look at these cute little monsters here. I **was looking** for souvenirs when I found these.

Das **past progressive** *ist die Verlaufsform der Vergangenheit. Mit dieser Zeitform drückst du aus, dass* **eine Handlung zu einem bestimmten Zeitpunkt in der Vergangenheit gerade ablief und** **noch nicht zu Ende** *war. Häufige Signalwörter hierfür sind* while *und* still.

○ *Du bildest das* **past progressive** *aus der Vergangenheitsform von* **be (was/were)** *und dem* **present participle** *(= Verb + -ing).*

Aussage:	The two men in Holly's picture **were wearing** kilts.
Verneinung:	They **weren't wearing** skirts.
Ergänzungsfrage:	What **was** the guy on the right **doing**?
Entscheidungsfrage mit Kurzantwort:	**Was** he **dancing** too? – No, he **wasn't**.

Die Zeitformen des Verbs — Grammar G

- Mit dem **past progressive** betonst du den Verlauf einer Handlung, die zu einem bestimmten Zeitpunkt in der Vergangenheit bereits angefangen hatte und noch nicht zu Ende war.

9 p.m. → → 7 a.m.	At 6 a.m. Holly **was** still **sleeping**.
6 a.m.	Um 6 Uhr schlief Holly noch.

- Du verwendest es auch, wenn sich in der Vergangenheit eine Handlung noch im Verlauf befand, als etwas Neues einsetzte. Diese neu eintretende Handlung steht dann im **simple past**.

Past progressive: gerade ablaufende Handlung	*Simple past:* neu eintretende Handlung
Holly **was looking for** souvenirs	when she **found** the Loch Ness monsters.
While Holly **was looking for** souvenirs,	she **found** the Loch Ness monsters.

❗ Das past progressive gibt es im Deutschen nicht. Du kannst es mit „gerade dabei sein, etwas zu tun" oder mit „während" wiedergeben.

> **English summary**
>
> You use the past progressive
>
> 1. to describe an action that was still happening at a certain time in the past.
> 2. to describe an action that was going on at a time when something else happened.
>
> *At 4 p.m. yesterday afternoon Gwen and Holly were walking around Glasgow. They were walking around Glasgow when it started to rain.*

4 How long have they been chatting?

→ SB 3, Unit 3

Die Verlaufsform des Perfekts
The present perfect progressive

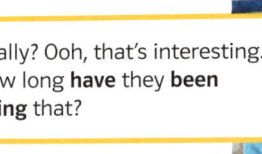

Did you know that Ethan and Amber **have been chatting** with each other online?

Really? Ooh, that's interesting. How long **have** they **been doing** that?

Oh, just for a few days. They'**ve been sending** each other messages since the weekend, I think.

nine 9

G Grammar — Die Zeitformen des Verbs

*Das **present perfect progressive** ist die Verlaufsform des present perfect.*
Mit dieser Zeitform drückst du aus, dass eine Handlung in der Vergangenheit begann, bis zum Zeitpunkt des Sprechens (also in die Gegenwart) hineinreicht und möglicherweise auch in der Zukunft noch andauern wird.

- Das **present perfect progressive** bildest du aus **have / has + been + present participle** (verb + -ing).

Aussage:	Amber **has been chatting** with Ethan online.
Verneinung:	She **hasn't been doing** her homework.
Ergänzungsfrage:	How long **has** she **been doing** that?
Entscheidungsfrage mit Kurzantwort:	**Have** they **been talking** to each other on the phone too? Yes, they **have**. / No, they **haven't**.

- Mit dem **present perfect** verbindest du die Vergangenheit mit der Gegenwart.
  Wie du schon weißt, verwendest du das **present perfect simple** (I have done), *um das **Ergebnis** einer vergangenen Handlung zu betonen.*
  Das **present perfect progressive** (I have been doing) verwendest du hingegen, um den **Verlauf** oder die **Dauer** der Handlung in den Vordergrund zu stellen.

  Vergleiche:

Gwen **has invited** Holly and Amber to Scotland.	Diese Handlung ist beendet; das Ergebnis steht im Vordergrund.
Gwen and her family **have been planning** things they can do together.	Diese Handlung dauert bis zum Zeitpunkt des Sprechens und möglicherweise darüber hinaus an; im Vordergrund steht die Handlung selbst.

- Oft verwendest du mit dem present perfect progressive eine Zeitangabe, die angibt, seit wann **(since)** oder wie lange **(for)** die Handlung schon andauert.

Mit **since** (seit, seitdem) gibst du den **Zeitpunkt** an, an dem eine Handlung begann.	z. B. since 1996; since 10 o'clock; since Monday; since last week; since August; since he moved to Scotland
Mit **for** (seit) gibst du den **Zeitraum** an, den eine Handlung bereits andauert.	z. B. for hours; for days; for weeks; for months; for years; for a long time

I have been …ing since …	
Gwen's uncle and aunt **have been living** in Scotland **since 1996**.	
	… wohnen schon seit 1996 in Schottland.
Amber **has been talking about** their trip to Scotland **since Gwen invited them**.	
	spricht schon davon, seitdem Gwen sie eingeladen hat.

Die Zeitformen des Verbs — Grammar G

I have been …ing for …	
Amber and Ethan **have been chatting** online **for a few days now**.	
	… unterhalten sich (jetzt schon) seit ein paar Tagen.
Amber **has been telling** Holly what to do **for years**.	
	… erzählt … schon seit Jahren / jahrelang …

❗ *Denke daran, dass es diese Zeitform im Deutschen nicht gibt. Wir benutzen stattdessen das **Präsens** und betonen die Dauer des Vorgangs mit **schon**.*

○ *Weitere Signalwörter für das* present perfect progressive *sind:* how long; recently *(in letzter Zeit);* all day / week / year *(den ganzen Tag …) sowie* all the time *(die ganze Zeit).*

❗ *Beachte, dass du das* present perfect progressive *wie alle Verlaufsformen **nur bei Tätigkeitsverben** verwenden kannst (z. B.* work, play, live*). Bei Verben, die keine Tätigkeit, sondern einen Zustand bezeichnen (z. B.* be, know, believe, see*) benutzt du das* present perfect simple, *z. B.* Gwen and Holly **have known** each other for a long time now.

❗ *Beachte, dass die unterschiedlichen* progressive*-Formen auch unterschiedlich verwendet werden.*

Present progressive:	Gwen is running.	Dies tut sie gerade.
Past progressive:	Gwen was running when …	Dies tat sie gerade, als …
Present perfect progressive:	Gwen has been running since / for …	Dies tut sie seit …

○ **English summary** ○

You use the present perfect progressive **(have / has + been + present participle)**

1. for an activity which began in the past, is still happening in the present and may still go on in the future.
2. to say how long an action has been happening.
You use **since** with a **point in time** (since 1996; since yesterday) and **for** with a **period of time** (for years; for a long time).

Amber and Holly have been fighting with each other again.

Ethan has been sending Amber messages since the weekend / for a few days now.

G Grammar — Die Zeitformen des Verbs

5 He hadn't finished his game
→ SB 3, Unit 4

Das Plusquamperfekt
The past perfect simple

Drake **wasn't** worried when he **heard** about the Spanish Armada …	because he **had fought** a lot of battles before.
Drake war nicht beunruhigt, als er von der spanischen Armada erfuhr,	*weil er (zuvor) schon viele Schlachten geschlagen hatte.*

Mit dem past perfect simple *betonst du, dass etwas **vor einem Zeitpunkt in der Vergangenheit** stattgefunden hat und abgeschlossen ist.*

- Das **past perfect simple** bildest du aus **had + past participle** (3. Verbform).

Aussage:	Drake **had seen** the Spanish Armada.
Verneinung:	But he **hadn't finished** his game of bowls.
Ergänzungsfrage:	Why **had** they **come**?
Entscheidungsfrage mit Kurzantwort:	**Had** they **come** to destroy his ships? Yes, they **had**.

Die Zeitformen des Verbs — Grammar G

○ Das **past perfect simple** spielt vor allem in literarischen Texten, Erzählungen und Berichten eine Rolle. Es steht meist in Verbindung mit dem **simple past**.
Mit dem **simple past** drückst du aus, was sich in der **Vergangenheit** ereignet hat. Für Handlungen oder Zustände, die noch **vor diesem Zeitpunkt der Vergangenheit** stattgefunden haben, verwendest du das **past perfect simple**.

simple past *(Vergangenheit)*	past perfect simple *(Vorvergangenheit)*
Before Elizabeth I **became** queen,	she **had said**: "I'll never marry."
When she **died** in 1603,	she **had been** queen for 45 years.

❗ Das Ereignis/die Handlung im **past perfect simple** kann auch am **Satzanfang** stehen.

past perfect simple *(Vorvergangenheit)*	simple past *(Vergangenheit)*
People in England **had** never **tasted** potatoes	before Walter Raleigh **brought** them back from America.
After Drake **had defeated** the Spanish,	he **became** a national hero.

❗ Wenn du in einer Erzählung oder in einem Bericht die Ereignisse der Reihe nach erzählst, benutzt du das **simple past**:
Elizabeth I **was** born in 1533 and **became** Queen of England in 1588 when she **was** 25 years old.
Blickst du bei deiner Erzählung jedoch auf ein Ereignis zurück, das zuvor stattgefunden hat und abgeschlossen ist, verwendest du das **past perfect simple**:
She **was** the daughter of Henry VIII and his second wife Anne Boleyn. But Elizabeth I never really **knew** her mother because she **had died** in 1536.

○ **English summary**

You use the **past perfect simple (had + past participle)** to show that one event happened before another in the past.

*Shakespeare took many of the ideas for his plays from stories which he **had read** at school.*

6 How long had they been doing that?

→ SB 4, Unit 3

Die Verlaufsform des Plusquamperfekts
The past perfect progressive

When Emilio arrived home, he felt tired. He **had been working** hard all day.

G Grammar — Die Zeitformen des Verbs

> *Das* **past perfect** *wird verwendet, um Vorzeitigkeit vor einem bestimmten Zeitpunkt in der Vergangenheit auszudrücken.*
> *Mit dem* **past perfect simple** *(I had done) betonst du* **das Ergebnis** *einer abgeschlossenen Handlung, z. B. Emilio felt tired. He* **had had** *a hard day.*
> *Mit dem* **past perfect progressive** *(I had been doing) betonst du den* **Verlauf** *oder die* **Dauer** *dieser Handlung, z. B. Emilio felt tired. He* **had been working** *hard all day.*

- *Das* **past perfect progressive** *bildest du aus* **had been** *+* **present participle** *(verb + -ing)*

Aussage:	He **had been listening**.
Verneinung:	He **hadn't been listening**.
Ergänzungsfrage:	How long **had** he **been listening**?
Entscheidungsfrage mit Kurzantwort:	**Had** he **been listening**? Yes, he **had**. / No, he **hadn't**.

- *Das* **past perfect progressive** *benutzt du für Handlungen, die vor einem Zeitpunkt in der Vergangenheit angefangen haben und bis zu diesem Zeitpunkt andauerten. Hierbei wird die Dauer der Handlung häufig durch eine Zeitangabe betont, z. B.* for ten years, since 2015, all day / week / year, all the time *usw.*

Past perfect progressive + *Zeitangabe*	*Vergangenheit*
Emilio **had been waiting** for 20 minutes … *wartete schon seit* …	before his first passenger arrived.
His second passenger **hadn't been sitting** in his taxi **for long** … *hatte noch nicht lange im Taxi gesessen* …	when he started to ask lots of questions.

- *Der Gebrauch des* **past perfect progressive** *ist mit der Verwendung des* **present perfect progressive** *vergleichbar. Die beschriebenen Handlungen dauern jedoch nicht bis in die Gegenwart an, sondern nur bis zu einem Zeitpunkt in der Vergangenheit.*

Present (now) ←←←←	Present perfect progressive
Emilio **is** tired	because he **has been driving** around New York all day.
Past (yesterday) ←←←	**Past perfect progressive**
Emilio **was** tired	because he **had been driving** around New York all day.

> ❗ *Beachte, dass du das* **past perfect progressive** *wie alle Verlaufsformen* **nur bei Tätigkeitsverben** *verwenden kannst (z. B.* wait, work, live*). Bei Verben, die keine Tätigkeit, sondern einen Zustand bezeichnen (z. B.* be, know, belong*) benutzt du das* **past perfect simple***, z. B.* Emilio had only been at the taxi stand for a few minutes when his next passenger got in.

Grammar G
Das Gerundium und der Infinitiv

> **English summary**
>
> You use the past perfect progressive to stress how long an activity continued before another event in the past happened. It is often used with an expression of time, e.g. *since, for, all day* etc.
>
> Last week Diego found a new assistant for his diner. He **had been looking for** help since the summer.

Das Gerundium und der Infinitiv

7 Living here isn't bad
→ SB 4, Unit 2

Das Gerundium
The gerund (verb + -ing)

Living in rural Pennsylvania isn't bad. But I really **miss seeing** my friends at home and I'm **scared of changing** too much. What's Pittsburgh like? I'm **thinking of coming** to visit soon. How about **meeting up** there?

Pittsburgh is amazing. I just **love being** here. It's really cool. But I still can't **get used to living** on the 22nd floor! I'm afraid I'm very busy here, so **meeting up** isn't easy right now.

Das **gerund** *(verb + -ing) ist eine Verbform, die es im Deutschen nicht gibt. Im Satz kann es verschiedene Funktionen haben. Es wird folgendermaßen verwendet:*
1. *als Subjekt* (**Living** here isn't …),
2. *als Objekt nach bestimmten Verben* (I miss **seeing** …),
3. *nach Präpositionen* (I'm scared of **changing** … / I'm thinking of **coming** … / How about **meeting** …).

- *Das* **gerund** *sieht aus wie das* present participle *(playing, taking, running) und wird genauso gebildet. Es gelten auch die gleichen Schreibregeln:*
  try + -ing → trying   liv**e** + -ing → li**v**ing   ge**t** + -ing → ge**tt**ing

- *Im Deutschen wird das* **gerund** *mit dem* **Infinitiv** *wiedergegeben:*
  I miss **seeing** my friends.   *Ich vermisse es, meine Freunde* **zu sehen**.
  Living here isn't bad.   *Es ist nicht schlecht hier* **zu leben**.

Grammar — Das Gerundium und der Infinitiv

a) *Das* **gerund** *als Subjekt des Satzes*

Meeting up isn't easy right now.	Sich zu treffen ist im Moment nicht einfach.
Finding new friends can be difficult.	Neue Freunde zu finden kann schwierig sein.
Living in America is awesome.	In Amerika zu leben ist toll.

- Als Subjekt des Satzes steht das **gerund** am Satzanfang und wird wie ein Nomen gebraucht.
- Es kann allein stehen (**Meeting up**), zusammen mit einem Nomen verwendet werden (**Finding new friends**) *und auch eine adverbiale Bestimmung bei sich haben* (**Living in America**).

b) *Das* **gerund** *als Objekt des Satzes nach bestimmten Verben*

Matt **enjoys**	**being** in Pittsburgh.	Matt ist gerne in Pittsburgh.
Sophie **didn't mind**	**moving** to America.	Sophie hatte nichts dagegen, nach Amerika umzuziehen.
Lena **keeps**	**thinking about** her friends in Germany.	Lena denkt immer wieder an ihre Freunde in Deutschland.
She **misses**	**hanging out** with them.	Sie vermisst es, Zeit mit ihnen zu verbringen.

- Als Objekt des Satzes steht **nach bestimmten Verben** das **gerund** *anstelle eines Infinitivs mit to, z. B.* Matt **enjoys being** in Pittsburgh *(nicht:* Matt enjoys to be …*).*
- Häufig sind es Verben, die allgemeine Vorlieben oder Abneigungen ausdrücken, wie enjoy, like, dislike, love, hate.
- Weitere Verben, nach denen ein **Verb** als **gerund** stehen **muss**, sind: keep, miss, imagine und suggest.

c) *Das* **gerund** *als Objekt nach Präpositionen*

1. *Adjektiv + Präposition +* **gerund**

Lena is **scared of**	**changing** too much.	Lena hat Angst davor, sich zu sehr zu verändern.
Sophie is **tired of**	**living** in the middle of nowhere.	Sophie hat es satt, am Ende der Welt zu wohnen.
Matt isn't **worried about**	**being** bored in Pittsburgh.	Matt macht sich keine Sorgen, dass er sich in Pittsburgh langweilen könnte.

- Weitere Verbindungen von Adjektiv + Präposition, nach denen ein **gerund** stehen **muss**, sind: good at, interested in, crazy about.

Das Gerundium und der Infinitiv — Grammar G

2. **Verb + Präposition + gerund**

Lena is **looking forward to**	**seeing** Matt again.	*Lena freut sich darauf, Matt wiederzusehen.*
But Matt doesn't **feel like**	**meeting** up with her.	*Aber Matt hat keine Lust, sich mit ihr zu treffen.*
He is **thinking of**	**inviting** Sophie to a baseball game.	*Er denkt darüber nach, Sophie zu einem Baseballspiel einzuladen.*

- *Weitere Verbindungen von Verb + Präposition, nach denen ein* **gerund** *steht, sind:*
  talk about, get used to, dream of, forgive somebody for, worry about.

❗ *Bei* look forward **to** *(sich freuen* ***auf****) und* get used **to** *(sich gewöhnen* ***an****) ist das* **to** *eine Präposition, die zum vorangestellten Verb gehört und auf die das* **gerund** *folgt:*
Sophie can't get used **to sharing** a room with her messy cousin.
She's looking forward **to moving** to Pittsburgh soon.

> **English summary**
>
> The gerund has the same form as the present participle: going, living etc. It can be used …
>
> 1. as the subject of the sentence.
> 2. as the object of the sentence after certain verbs, e.g. *enjoy, like, hate, imagine, mind*.
> 3. after prepositions
>   a) adjective + preposition + gerund
>   b) verb + preposition + gerund
>
> **Living** in rural Pennsylvania is OK.
> Lena doesn't mind **being** there.
>
> She isn't worried about **having to** travel for two hours to get there.
> She's looking forward to **going** to the mall.

8 That's the worst thing to do! → SB 4, Unit 2

Der Infinitiv mit und ohne to
The infinitive with and without *to*

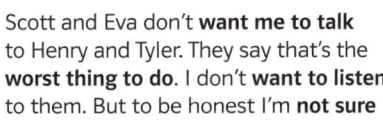

Scott and Eva don't **want me to talk** to Henry and Tyler. They say that's the **worst thing to do**. I don't **want to listen** to them. But to be honest I'm **not sure what to do**.

I'm glad I don't have your problems, Matt, but mine aren't much better, you know. I **can** never **meet** friends after school because my parents always **make me come** straight home. They won't **let me do** anything.

G Grammar — Das Gerundium und der Infinitiv

> Der **Infinitiv** ist die Grundform des Verbs. Im Englischen findet sich der Infinitiv in zwei Formen: **mit to** *(to be, to go, to play)* und **ohne to** *(be, go, play)*.
> Der **Infinitiv mit to** steht nach zahlreichen Verben, Adjektiven und Nomen.
> Der **Infinitiv ohne to** wird vor allem nach Hilfsverben *(can, must, should)*, aber auch nach anderen Verben wie let oder make + Objekt gebraucht.

a) Der *Infinitiv mit* to nach bestimmten Verben

Would you **like**	**to watch** the movie on TV this evening?
No, I'**d prefer**	**to go** to the movie theater.
OK. I'll **try**	**to get** some tickets.

- Verben auf die der *Infinitiv mit* to folgt, können in folgende Gruppen unterteilt werden:
  1. **Wünsche und Absichten**, z. B. want, would like, hope, decide, expect, offer, plan, promise
  2. **Vorlieben**, die sich auf konkrete Situationen beziehen, z. B. choose, prefer
  3. **Versuche** oder **Bemühungen**, z. B. try, learn, manage.

b) Der *Infinitiv mit* to nach Verb + Fragewort oder nach whether

Direkte Frage	Indirekte Frage	mit can, should, must, have to / mit Infinitiv + to
Where do I have to go?	Matt doesn't **know**	where he has to go. / where **to go**.
Who can I ask?	He **isn't sure**	who he can ask. / who **to ask**.
Should I sit with Henry and Tyler?	He **wonders**	**if** he should sit with Henry and Tyler. / **whether to sit** with Henry and Tyler.

- Nach **know, be sure, decide, wonder** + *Fragewort* (what, when, where, which, whether) steht der *Infinitiv mit* to oft anstelle einer indirekten Frage (mit can, should, must, have to).

❗ Bei Entscheidungsfragen wird bei der Infinitivkonstruktion if *(ob)* durch **whether** ersetzt.

c) Der *Infinitiv mit* to nach Superlativen

Hauptsatz + Relativsatz	Hauptsatz + Infinitiv mit to
You are the first person who has said that.	You are **the first** (person) **to say** that.
I was the only one who ordered meat.	I was **the only one to order** meat.
That's the worst thing that you can do.	That's **the worst thing to do**.

- Nach **the first, the last, the only one** und nach **Superlativen** (the worst thing, the most important thing) ersetzt der *Infinitiv mit* to einen Relativsatz.

Das Gerundium und der Infinitiv **Grammar** G

d) Der *Infinitiv mit* to nach Verb + Objekt

Verb	Objekt	Infinitiv mit to
Henry and Tyler **want**	people	**to think** about sweatshops and child labor.
They **would like**	them	**to join** their protest at the mall.
Scott and Eva **expect**	Matt	**to ignore** them.

- Auf die folgenden Verben kann die Verbindung von **Objekt** + *Infinitiv mit* to folgen:
  ask *(bitten)*, expect, prefer, tell, warn, want *und* would like.

❗ Nach want *(wollen, dass) und* would like *(möchten, dass) darfst du keinen Nebensatz mit* that *anschließen. Vergleiche:*

Matt: Scott and Eva want **me to drop** Henry and Tyler.
Scott und Eva wollen, **dass ich** Henry und Tyler fallen lasse.

e) Der *Infinitiv ohne* to nach let und make + Objekt

Verb	Objekt	Infinitiv ohne to
Sophie's parents won't **let**	her	**meet** her friends after school.
They **make**	her	**come** straight home.
Do your parents **let**	you	**do** what you want?
Or do they **make**	you	**come** home early too?

- Nach make + Objekt *(veranlassen, zwingen) und* let + Objekt *(zulassen, erlauben) wird der* **Infinitiv ohne** to *gebraucht.*

English summary

The infinitive with *to* is used …

1. after certain verbs, e.g. *want, expect, decide, would like / would prefer*
2. after certain verbs + questions words
3. after superlatives *(the first / last / only one / the best thing)*
4. after *want, would like, expect, ask, tell* + object

Sophie's parents always **want to know** where she is. They**'d like to take** control of her life.
Sophie **isn't sure what to do**.
She's **the only one to have** parents who are so strict.
She **would like them to relax** more.

The infinitive without *to* is used …

1. after modal verbs
   (can, should, must, have to)

They **should trust** her.

Grammar — Das Gerundium und der Infinitiv

9 Gerund or infinitive: It depends on the meaning
Das gerund oder der Infinitiv mit to: Bedeutungsunterschiede

→ SB 4, Unit 2

Dad, I've got a problem with my computer. I've **tried turning** it off and **starting** it up again, but that hasn't worked.

I'm sorry, Sophie. I'm really busy at the moment. But I'll **try to find** some time this afternoon. Maybe I can help you then.

*Nach einigen wenigen Verben (forget, go on, mean, remember, stop, try) wird je nach Bedeutung entweder ein **gerund** oder ein **Infinitiv mit to** verwendet.*

a) *Nach go on, mean, stop und try hängt die* **Bedeutung des Verbs** *davon ab, ob ihm ein* **gerund** *oder ein* **Infinitiv mit to** *folgt.*

to go on doing sth *etwas fortsetzen / weitermachen*	to go on to do sth *etwas anschließend machen*
They **went on talking**. Sie redeten weiter.	Then they **went on to talk about** child labor. Anschließend sprachen sie über Kinderarbeit.

to mean doing sth *bedeuten*	to mean to do sth *wollen, beabsichtigen*
That **means walking**. Das bedeutet, dass wir laufen müssen.	I **meant to send** you a text, but I forgot. Ich wollte dir eine SMS schicken, aber …

to stop doing sth *aufhören, etwas zu tun*	to stop to do something *anhalten, um etwas Neues zu tun*
Stop shouting! Hör auf, zu schreien!	Let's **stop to have** a drink. Lasst uns anhalten, um etwas zu trinken.

to try doing sth *eine Methode ausprobieren*	to try to do sth *eine konkrete Handlung ausprobieren*
If you can't sleep, **try counting** sheep. … probier's mal mit Schäfchen zählen.	I **tried to sleep** in the car, but it wasn't possible. Ich habe versucht, im Auto zu schlafen, aber …

Das Passiv **Grammar** G

b) *Nach* remember *und* forget *steht das* **gerund** *für eine Handlung, die* **bereits stattgefunden hat** *und an die man sich erinnert. Der* **Infinitiv mit to** *weist hingegen auf eine Handlung hin, die* **beabsichtigt ist** *und* **noch bevorsteht**.

to remember doing sth *sich erinnern an*	to remember to do sth *daran denken, etwas zu tun*
Sophie can't **remember visiting** London. She was too young. *Sophie kann sich nicht daran erinnern, dass sie London besucht hat. …*	Please **remember to learn** the irregular verbs for the test. *Denkt bitte daran, die unregelmäßigen Verben für den Test zu lernen.*

to forget doing sth *vergessen, wie man etwas getan hat*	to forget to do sth *vergessen, etwas zu tun*
Lena will never **forget having to say goodbye** to her friends in Hamburg. *Lena wird nie vergessen, wie sie sich von ihren Freunden … verabschieden musste.*	Please don't **forget to tidy** your room before your friends arrive. *Vergiss nicht, dein Zimmer aufzuräumen, bevor deine Freunde kommen.*

❗ *Nach* to begin, to start *und* to like *(im Sinne von „genießen") kann sowohl das* **gerund** *als auch der* **Infinitiv mit to** *stehen. Die Bedeutung ist in beiden Fällen gleich!*
It started to rain.   It started raining.
I like to go to the movie theater.   I like going to the movie theater.

○ **English summary** ○

Some English verbs such as *forget, go on, mean, remember, stop* and *try* can be followed by a gerund or by an infinitive with *to*, but with a change in meaning.

We **stopped to buy** some eggs from the farm.
We've **stopped buying** them from the supermarket.

Das Passiv

10 **Is Haggis made with meat?** → SB 3, Unit 3

Das Passiv
The passive

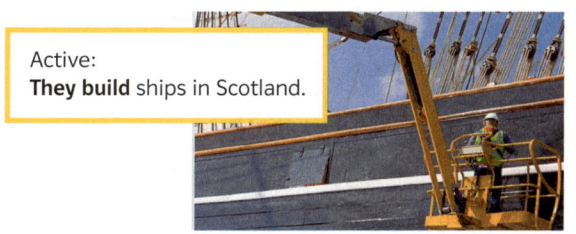

Active:
They build ships in Scotland.

Passive:
Ships **are built** in Scotland.

twenty-one **21**

G Grammar — Das Passiv

> Du benutzt das Passiv, wenn der Ausführende einer Handlung unwichtig oder nicht bekannt ist. Damit rückt die Handlung selbst in den Vordergrund.
> Das Passiv wird häufig in Zeitungsberichten, Sachtexten und technischen Beschreibungen verwendet.

- Das Passiv bildest du mit einer Form von **be** in der jeweiligen Zeitform und dem **past participle** des Vollverbs (infinitive + -ed oder unregelmäßige Form).

Zeitform	Form von be + past participle	Beispiel
simple present	am / is / are + past participle	Haggis **is made** with meat. … wird … gemacht.
simple past	was / were + past participle	The house **was built** 20 years ago. … wurde vor … gebaut.
present perfect simple	have / has been + past participle	Whisky **has been produced** in Scotland for 500 years. … wird seit … hergestellt.

❗ Im Deutschen verwendest du für das Passiv eine Form von „werden".

- Wenn du in einem Passivsatz sagen möchtest, von wem die Handlung ausgeführt wird, verwendest du die Präposition **by** (auf Deutsch: von). Du entscheidest im Einzelfall, ob diese Zusatzinformation wichtig ist oder nicht:
  Gaelic **is only spoken by** a few people today.
  Gälisch **wird** heute nur **von** wenigen Menschen **gesprochen**.
  Der Ausführende der Handlung wird **by-agent** genannt.

- Wenn du einen Aktivsatz in einen Passivsatz umwandelst, musst du Folgendes beachten:
  1. Das Objekt des Aktivsatzes wird zum Subjekt im Passivsatz. Aus **Objektpronomen** werden **Subjektpronomen:** me, you, him, her, it, us, you, them → I, you, he, she, it, we, you, they.
  2. Die Aktivform des Verbs wird zur Passivform, indem du die passende Form von **be** mit dem **past participle** des Aktivverbs verbindest (take → are taken).
  3. Das Subjekt des Aktivsatzes wird nicht genannt. Ist der Ausführende der Handlung jedoch für den Kontext wichtig, wird das Subjekt mit dem **by-agent** angefügt.

Aktiv:	Passiv:
People all over the world **have read** the Sherlock Holmes' stories.	The Sherlock Holmes' stories **have been read by** people all over the world.
The Scottish author Sir Arthur Conan Doyle **wrote** them.	They **were written by** the Scottish author Sir Arthur Conan Doyle.
Every year thousands of fans **visit** his famous home in Baker Street.	Every year his famous home in Baker Street **is visited by** thousands of fans.

❗ Die Zeitform im Aktivsatz und im Passivsatz bleibt gleich.

Direkte und indirekte Rede **Grammar** G

> **English summary**
>
> You form the passive voice with a form of **be** and the **past participle**.
>
> 1. You use the active to stress what the subject does.
> 2. You use the passive to stress what is done. Often you don't know who has done the action, or you think this is not important.
> 3. If it's important to say who does the action, you use the **by-agent**.
>
> *The electric clock **was invented by** the Scotsman Alexander Bain.*

Direkte und indirekte Rede

11 You told us there was free wifi! → SB 4, Unit 1

Aussagen in der indirekten Rede
Statements in indirect speech

Direct speech:
Steve's parents: We're worried about Steve, Ms Woodruff. He **can't** live without **his** phone. He**'s** addicted to it.

Indirect speech:
Your parents told me (that) they **were** worried about you. They said (that) you **couldn't** live without **your** phone and they thought (that) you **were** addicted to it.

Wenn du wiedergeben möchtest, was ein anderer dir mitgeteilt hat, verwendest du gewöhnlich nicht die direkte, sondern die indirekte Rede.

G Grammar — Direkte und indirekte Rede

- *Wie du schon weißt, besteht die indirekte Rede aus einem* **Einführungssatz** *(Hauptsatz) (They told me … / They said …), und einem* **Nebensatz**, *der mit oder ohne that eingeleitet werden kann (… that they were worried about you).*
- *Anders als im Deutschen steht zwischen dem Einführungssatz und dem Nebensatz* **kein** *Komma.*
- *Wenn du eine Aussage in der indirekten Rede wiedergibst, musst du Personalpronomen und Possessivbegleiter anpassen (we → they; his → your).*
- *Steht das Verb im Einleitungssatz im* **simple present**, *wird die Zeitform aus der direkten Rede in den Nebensatz der indirekten Rede übernommen.*
- *Steht das Verb im Einleitungssatz jedoch im* **simple past**, *ändert sich die Zeitform im Nebensatz folgendermaßen:*

Direkte Rede Direct speech	*Indirekte Rede* Indirect speech
simple present → Steve's parents: We **are** worried about Steve.	**simple past** Steve's parents told Ms Woodruff that they **were** worried about Steve.
present progressive → We think he **is spending** too much time on his phone.	**past progressive** They thought he **was spending** too much time on his phone.
present perfect → I **have tried** to take his phone away, …	**past perfect** His mum explained that she **had tried** to take his phone away, …
simple past → … but that **didn't work**.	**past perfect** … but that **hadn't worked**.
can → We **can't** help him.	**could** They said they **couldn't** help him.
will → Ms Woodruff: OK, I**'ll** talk to him.	**would** Ms Woodruff promised that she **would** talk to him.

English summary

You use indirect speech when you want to report what somebody has said.

When the reporting verb is in the simple past (He said that … / They told her that … / She thought …), the verbs used in the original speech usually move one tense further back (present → past; past → past perfect simple; will → would; can → could).

Steve: *I'm on the ferry to Calais. I'll call you back later.*

Steve told Eddie that he was on the ferry to Calais and that he'd call him back later.

Direkte und indirekte Rede

Grammar G

12 Steve's blog
→ SB 4, Unit 1

Zeit- und Ortsangaben in der indirekten Rede
Expressions of time and place in indirect speech

Friday morning:
Steve: We **had** horsemeat for dinner **yesterday**.

Friday afternoon:
Steve told me that they **had had** horsemeat for dinner **yesterday**.

A few days later:
Last Friday Steve told me that they **had had** horsemeat for dinner **the day before**.

Wenn die indirekte Rede sich auf eine Aussage aus der Vergangenheit bezieht, musst du auch die Zeit- und Ortsangaben im Satz verändern.

- *Die Zeitangaben ändern sich folgendermaßen:*

today → that day	this evening → that evening
tomorrow → the next day	three days ago → three days before
yesterday → the day before	last week / year → the week / year before
next year → the following year	now → then

- *Auch Ortsangaben ändern sich, wenn die Aussage später an einem anderen Ort wiedergegeben wird:* here → there.

- *Weitere Wörter, die meist in der indirekten Rede verändert werden, um sie dem Standpunkt des Berichtenden anzupassen, sind:* this → that; these → those; come → go *und* bring → take.

It's quite cold over **here**.
This is unusual for the time of year. So when you **come**, you shouldn't forget to **bring** some warm clothes,
Michel Lebrun

Listen boys and girls,
I've had an e-mail from Monsieur Lebrun. He said that it was quite cold over **there**. **That** was unusual for the time of year. So when we **go**, we shouldn't forget to **take** some warm clothes.

twenty-five 25

G Grammar — Direkte und indirekte Rede

> **English summary**
>
> In indirect speech, adverbs of time often change too, e. g. **today → that day**, **yesterday → the day before** etc.
> But if you report something **on the same day** as it was said, the adverbs of time **don't** change.
> Other words that you may need to change are:
> this → that; here → there; come → go; bring → take.
>
> Steve: *I'm going to France tomorrow.*
>
> (the same day)
> Steve said he was going to France tomorrow.
>
> (a week later):
> Steve said he was going to France the next day.

13 He asked me what the purpose of my visit was → SB 4, Unit 1
Fragen in der indirekten Rede
Questions in indirect speech

Direct question:	Indirect speech:
Steve's grandma: When **is** your flight, Rafiq?	Grandma **asked** me when my flight **was**.
How **are** you **getting** to the airport?	She **asked** me how I **was getting** to the airport.
Have you **weighed** your suitcase?	She **asked** me if I **had weighed** my suitcase.
Are you nervous about the trip?	She **asked** me if I **was** nervous about the trip.
Did you **find** a nice present for Aunt Sadia?	She **wanted to know** if I **had found** a nice present for Aunt Sadia.
When **will** you be back?	She **wanted to know** when I **would** be back.

Fragen werden in der indirekten Rede als Aussagesätze wiedergegeben.

- Das Verb im **Einführungssatz** (Hauptsatz) muss deutlich machen, dass es sich um eine indirekte Frage handelt (Grandma **asked** me … / She **wanted to know** …).

- Das Fragewort (what, when, where, why …) wird in der indirekten Frage als Bindewort zwischen Haupt- und Nebensatz übernommen. Steht **kein** Fragewort, leitest du den Nebensatz mit **if** ein.

- Die Wortstellung im Nebensatz ist die gleiche wie in einem Aussagesatz: Das **Subjekt** steht immer **vor** dem **Verb**. Umschreibungen mit do / does / did fallen weg.

Direkte und indirekte Rede **Grammar** G

- *Wie bei indirekten Aussagesätzen werden bei indirekten Fragen die Zeitformen meist um eine Zeitstufe zurückverschoben, wenn das Einleitungsverb im* simple past *steht.*

> **English summary**
>
> 1. If you report questions that begin with a question word (what, when, how …), you use **asked / wanted to know + question word**.
> 2. If there is no question word, you use **if**.
> 3. The word order in indirect questions is the same as in statements: Subject – Verb.
> 4. The verb in the direct question moves one tense further back.
>
> Steve's grandma: *How long is the flight to Dhaka?*
> Grandma **wanted to know how long** the flight to Dhaka **was**.
>
> Steve's grandma: *Will you be able to sleep on the plane?*
> **She asked Rafiq if** he **would** be able to sleep on the plane.

14 He told me to go into a side room

→ SB 4, Unit 1

Befehle, Aufforderungen und Bitten in der indirekten Rede
Commands and requests in indirect speech

Direct command / request:	Indirect command / request:
Steve's grandma: Don't spend all your money in the first week.	She **told** him (Rafiq) **not to spend** all his money in the first week.
Please send me some photos from Bangladesh.	Grandma **asked** him (Rafiq) **to send** her some photos from Bangladesh.

> *Befehle, Aufforderungen und Bitten werden in der indirekten Rede als Infinitivkonstruktion mit* **to** *oder* **not to** *wiedergegeben.*

- *In der indirekten Rede verwendest du meist* **tell somebody to do something** *für Befehle und Aufforderungen und* **ask somebody to do something** *für Bitten.*

- *Enthält der Befehlssatz ein Verbot (also eine Verneinung), wird* **don't** *zu* **not to** *(Don't shout → … not to shout).*

- *Dem Einleitungsverb* (told, asked) **folgt** *kein Nebensatz, sondern ein* **Personenobjekt + to-Infinitiv** *(She asked* **Rafiq to send** *…).*

- *Wird* **kein** *Eigenname genannt, verwendest du ein* **Pronomen** *in der* **Objektform** *(me, you, him, her, us, them) (She asked* **him** *…).*

❗ *Beachte, dass es hier keine Zeitverschiebung gibt, da der Befehl selbst durch einen Infinitiv wiedergegeben wird.*
Für weitere Verben im Satz gelten jedoch die Regeln für indirekte Aussagesätze.
Grandma: **Don't spend** all your money on things you **don't** need.
Grandma told Rafiq **not to spend** all his money on things he **didn't** need.

Grammar — Satz und Satzgefüge

> **English summary**
>
> In indirect speech, you use **to tell somebody (not) to do something** for indirect commands and **to ask somebody (not) to do something** for indirect requests.
>
> Flight attendant: *Fasten your seatbelt, please, and don't use your phone during take-off and landing.*
> The flight attendant **asked** Rafiq **to fasten** his seatbelt and **told** him **not to use** his phone during take-off and landing.

Satz und Satzgefüge

15 The boy who … / Diego, who …   → SB 4, Unit 3

Notwendige und nicht-notwendige Relativsätze
Defining and non-defining relative clauses

Diego is the boy **who took us around New York**. He showed us sights in New York **(which) you would never find in a guidebook**.

Diego, **who knows New York like the back of his hand**, showed the two girls some great places. All the sights were amazing, but Rockefeller Center, **which they visited last**, was just awesome.

*Relativsätze sind Nebensätze, die ihr **Bezugswort** im Hauptsatz*
a) *näher bestimmen* (**the boy** who took us around New York) *oder*
b) *zusätzlich beschreiben* (**Diego**, who knows New York like the back of his hand, …).
Im Englischen nennt man diese zwei Arten von Relativsätzen
defining *und* **non-defining relative clauses**.

a) Defining relative clauses

Two girls **who / that are spending the day in New York** visit a diner.
A boy **(who / that) they meet there** takes them on a tour of the city.
Some of the **sights (which / that) he shows them** are amazing.

- **Defining relative clauses** bestimmen ihr vorangestelltes **Bezugswort** im Hauptsatz näher. Sie legen fest, wer oder was gemeint ist. Ohne den Relativsatz wäre in den obigen Beispielen nicht klar, von welchen beiden Mädchen, von welchem Jungen oder von welchen Sehenswürdigkeiten genau die Rede ist.

- Relativsätze, die ihr Bezugswort näher bestimmen, stehen **ohne Komma**. Beim Sprechen macht man keine Pause.

- **Defining relative clauses** werden durch Relativpronomen wie **who** oder **that** (bei Personen) und **which** oder **that** (bei Sachen) eingeleitet, wenn sie das Subjekt im Relativsatz sind. Sind die Relativpronomen who, which, that *das Objekt im Relativsatz, können sie weggelassen werden* (a boy (**who / that**) they meet …; some of the sights (**that**) he shows …). Diese Relativsätze nennt man **contact clauses**.

b) **Non-defining relative clauses**

Rylee and Lea, who are spending the day in New York, visit a diner.
Diego, who they meet there, takes them on a tour of the city.
At **Rockefeller Center**, which they visit last, they have a scary experience.

- Bei **non-defining relative clauses** ist das vorangestellte **Bezugswort bereits definiert**. Auch ohne den Relativsatz bleibt klar, wer oder was gemeint ist: Rylee and Lea, Diego und das Rockefeller Center. Die Relativsätze bestimmen daher ihr Bezugswort **nicht** näher. Sie enthalten lediglich eine zusätzliche oder ergänzende Information, die ebenso gut in Klammern stehen oder entfallen könnte, ohne dass die Aussage im Hauptsatz verändert wird.

- Relativsätze, die Zusatzinformationen enthalten, werden vom Hauptsatz immer **durch Kommas abgetrennt**. Beim Sprechen wird eine Pause gemacht.

- Im Gegensatz zu defining relative clauses beginnen **non-defining relative clauses immer mit einem Relativpronomen**: Für Personen verwendet man **who**. Für Dinge verwendet man **which**. Das Relativpronomen **that** ist in einem **non-defining relative clause** nicht möglich.

> **English summary**
>
> There are two types of relative clauses: **defining** and **non-defining**.
>
> 1. Defining relative clauses tell you which person or thing the speaker is talking about.
>   **No comma** is used between the noun and the relative clause.
>
>   Lea is a German girl **who / that** comes from Berlin.
>
> 2. Non-defining relative clauses are used after nouns that are definite already. They give extra information about a person or thing.
>   You always need a **comma** to separate the main clause from the relative clause.
>
>   Lea, **who** is German, is Rylee's cousin from Berlin.
>
> 3. Non-defining relative clauses always begin with a relative pronoun. You use **who** for people and **which** for things. You **never** use **that**.
>
>   They walked to the Alvin Ailey Dance Studio, **which** is close to Central Park.

G Grammar — Satz und Satzgefüge

16 If you look at a map of Great Britain, you'll find Cornwall in the far west.

→ SB 3, Unit 1

Bedingungssätze Typ 1
Conditional clauses type 1

If you **like** beaches and fishing harbours, you'**ll find** that Cornwall is just the right place for you.

Well, you **can** go fishing **if** we **go** to Cornwall. What do you think?

Mit dem Bedingungssatz Typ 1 drückst du aus, was unter einer bestimmten Bedingung passieren wird. Der Sprecher hält die Bedingung für erfüllbar. Es ist also wahrscheinlich, dass die Folge eintritt.

- Der Bedingungssatz Typ 1 besteht aus einem **if-Satz** (Nebensatz) und einem Hauptsatz. Im **if-Satz** drückst du die Bedingung aus, im Hauptsatz sagst du, was passiert oder passieren kann, falls diese Bedingung erfüllt wird.

- Im **if-Satz** verwendest du das **simple present**, im **Hauptsatz** das **will future**.

Bedingung im if-Satz: simple present	Folge im Hauptsatz: will future
If you **look** at a map,	you**'ll see** that Cornwall is on the Atlantic Ocean.
If the friends **visit** Dave in Cornwall,	they **won't get** bored.

- Neben dem **will future** kannst du im **Hauptsatz** häufig auch die **Modalverben** (can, must, should + infinitive) oder den **Imperativ** verwenden.

if-Satz: simple present	Hauptsatz: Modalverb + infinitive oder Imperativ
If you **aren't** into sports,	you **can** go to a museum. (Möglichkeit)
If you **want** to learn about the environment,	you **should** visit the Eden Project. (Ratschlag)
If you **go** to Cornwall,	**try** real Cornish food. (Ratschlag / Aufforderung)

Bedingungssätze können entweder mit dem **if-Satz** oder mit dem **Hauptsatz** beginnen:
If you look at a map of Great Britain, you**'ll** find Cornwall in the far west.
You**'ll** find Cornwall in the far west **if** you look at a map of Great Britain. (*kein Komma vor if!*)

| Satz und Satzgefüge | **Grammar** | **G** |

❗ *Verwechsle nicht* **if** *(wenn/falls = Bedingung) mit* **when** *(wenn = zeitlicher Zusammenhang)!*
If we go on a beach holiday, I'll try surfing.
Wenn/Falls wir einen Strandurlaub machen, versuche ich zu surfen.
We'll see Dave **when** he visits his granny in London.
Wir werden Dave treffen, wenn er seine Großmutter in London besucht.

There's a teacher from Scotland at your school. In the next holidays he wants to travel around Germany. Tell him what he can and should do.

Example: If you go to Berlin, you can visit the Brandenburg Gate.
If you go to Leipzig, you should try "Leipziger Lerche".
If you visit Frankfurt, you'll see lots of tall buildings.

17 **They wouldn't worry if they didn't care.** → SB 3, Unit 2

Bedingungssätze Typ 2
Conditional clauses type 2

If I **had** the choice, I **would drop out of** school.

Mit dem Bedingungssatz Typ 2 drückst du aus, was unter einer bestimmten Bedingung passieren könnte. Der Sprecher hält diese Bedingung für nicht oder nicht so einfach erfüllbar.
Es ist also (zur Zeit) eher unwahrscheinlich, dass die Folge eintritt.

I know you want to become a famous singer. But **if** you **didn't think about** singing and dancing all the time, you **would have** better marks. **If** you **had** better marks, Mum and Dad **would support** you. So **if** I **were** you, I **would listen** to them and try harder at school.

thirty-one **31**

G Grammar — Satz und Satzgefüge

- Für die Bedingung im **if-Satz** verwendest du das **simple past**, für die Folge im **Hauptsatz** **would(n't) / could(n't) + infinitive**.
  Die entsprechende Kurzform von would lautet 'd (I'd, you'd, he'd …).

Bedingung im if-Satz: simple past	Folge im Hauptsatz: (would / could + infinitive)
If Jay **had** the choice,	he **would** / he**'d drop out of** school.
Wenn Jay die Wahl hätte, würde er die Schule abbrechen.	
If Jay **didn't have to** go to school,	he **could sing and dance** all day.
Wenn Jay nicht zur Schule gehen müsste, könnte er den ganzen Tag singen und tanzen.	
If I **looked** as good as Shahid,	I**'d work** as a model too.
Wenn ich so gut aussehen würde wie Shahid, würde ich auch als Model arbeiten.	
If I **were** Jay,	I**'d take** Shahid's advice.
Wenn ich Jay wäre, würde ich Shahids Rat annehmen.	

- Nach I / he / she / it kannst du **was** oder **were** verwenden.
  If I were / was rich, I'd …
  If he / she / it were / was famous, he'd …

⚠ Achte darauf, dass du **would** nur für die **Folge im Hauptsatz** verwendest! Die **Bedingung** im **if-Satz** steht immer im **simple past**.
  If Shahid **didn't work** as a model, he **wouldn't** have so much money.
  Wenn Shahid **nicht** als Model **arbeiten würde**, **würde** er nicht so viel Geld haben.

> **English summary**
>
> A conditional sentence has two parts: an **if-clause** and a **main clause**.
>
> - You use **type 1** when the **action in the if-clause** is **possible** and **probable**.
>   The verb in the **if-clause** is in the **simple present**; the verb in the **main clause** is in the **will future**: *If you make the right decisions now, you'll have more choices later.*
> - You use **type 2** when the **action in the if-clause** is **possible** but **not probable**.
>   The verb in the **if-clause** is in the **simple past**; the verb in the **main clause** is in the **conditional** tense: *If I had a million pounds, I'd travel the world.*

18 If I hadn't talked so much

→ SB 3, Unit 4

Bedingungssätze Typ 3
Conditional clauses type 3

Mit dem Bedingungssatz Typ 3 drückst du aus, was passiert wäre (oder hätte passieren können), wenn eine bestimmte Bedingung in der Vergangenheit eingetreten wäre.

Oh no! I'm really stupid! **If** I **hadn't talked** so much, **I wouldn't have lost** the others. But why have they turned their phones off? **If** they **hadn't done** that, **I could have rung** them.

- *Im Gegensatz zu den Bedingungssätzen Typ 1 und Typ 2 beschreibst du mit Typ 3 eine Situation, die sich nicht mehr verwirklichen lässt. Da die Bedingung in der Vergangenheit liegt, bleibt sie* **unerfüllbar**.

- *Für die Bedingung im* **if-Satz** *verwendest du das* **past perfect simple**, *für die Folge im* **Hauptsatz** **would(n't) / could(n't) have + past participle**.

Nicht mehr erfüllbare Bedingung im if-Satz: past perfect simple	*Folge im Hauptsatz:* would / could / should have + past participle
If Jay **had stayed** with his friends,	he **wouldn't have found out** so much about life in Victorian Britain.
If he **hadn't got lost**,	he **would / he'd have missed** all the cool stories.
If Jay's friends **hadn't turned off** their mobile phones,	they **could have helped** him.

English summary

You use a conditional sentence **type 3** when the **action in the if-clause** is **no longer possible** because the situation took place in the past and you cannot change what has already happened.
The verb in the **if-clause** is in the **past perfect simple**; the verb in the **main clause** is in the conditional perfect (**would have + past participle**): *If Jay hadn't joined the Victorian tour, he wouldn't have found a pipe for his calendar.*

Useful phrases

Inhalt

Es ist nicht immer leicht, in einer anderen Sprache die richtigen Sätze parat zu haben. Auf den folgenden Seiten findest du die *Useful phrases* aus Green Line 3 und 4 unter den wichtigsten Themen zusammengefasst wieder. Sie helfen dir dabei, in bestimmten Situationen genau die richtigen Worte zu finden!

Inhalt

Talk about people and places

36	1	How to talk about interests and personalities
36	2	How to talk about friends who get into trouble
36	3	How to talk about your own experiences with people's behaviour
36	4	How to talk about what you look for in others
37	5	How to talk and write about places
37	6	How to describe places for a quiz

Talk about different kinds of texts

37	7	How to talk about stories and legends
37	8	How to talk about poems
38	9	How to express your opinion about news reports / articles
38	10	How to talk about fictional texts
38	11	How to talk about the main characters in a drama
38	12	How to talk about graphic novels
38	13	How to talk about blog posts

Talk about visuals

39	14	How to describe cartoons
39	15	How to talk about photos
40	16	How to describe and analyze pictures
40	17	How to write a film rating

How to argue and discuss

40	18	How to compromise
41	19	How to persuade someone to change their behavior / express an attitude

Inhalt **Useful phrases** P

How to get along in everyday situations

41	20	How to talk about things to do in the country
42	21	How to make dialogues at the travel agent's
42	22	How to keep the ball bouncing (doing small talk)
43	23	How to break the ice

How to prepare and present different projects

43	24	How to tell a travel story
43	25	How to write a text for the yearbook
44	26	How to conduct a podcast interview

Talk about different topics

44	27	How to talk about different times in history
44	28	How to talk about rules at your school

thirty-five 35

Talk about people and places

1 How to talk about interests and personalities → SB 3, 27

A body smart / picture smart / music smart / logic smart / … person
… is good with his / her hands / body / imagination / …
… is good at doing / showing / using / creating / explaining / teaching / …
… knows how to use … / play … / talk … / communicate / compete / …
… is creative / imaginative / confident / …
… likes to … / needs to … / feels … / understands … / …
A … smart person would probably be a good teacher / doctor / …

Take turns to talk about the qualities of a body smart / picture smart / … person.

2 How to talk about friends who get into trouble → SB 3, 38

- One of my friends always gets into trouble for telling lies / making nasty comments / …
- My friend / cousin breaks the rules at home / at school / in our team / …
- There's always trouble when …
- I know somebody who always goes too far to be the best / to be popular / …
- He / She likes to start fights / tease people / …

What kind of trouble have your brothers / sisters / cousins / friends got into before?
Was it big trouble, or not so big? Tell a partner about it.

3 How to talk about your own experiences with people's behaviour → SB 4, 22

Just imagine what happened to me when … | I saw something really funny / strange / odd when … | I was really surprised. | I couldn't believe my eyes / ears. | I didn't understand what was going on. | Well, I guess every country has its own customs. | For me, it looked like good / bad behaviour, but then I realised …

Can you remember a situation in which someone behaved differently to what you'd normally expect (in Germany or in another country)? Tell your partner about what happened. How did you feel about it? How did you react?

4 How to talk about what you look for in others → SB 4, 55

- I look for … in a friend / boyfriend / girlfriend.
- The person should have / be …
- The most important thing to me is …
- It's attractive if the person is / has …

With a partner, talk about what you find attractive in others.

Talk about different kinds of texts | **Useful phrases** | **P**

5 How to talk and write about places → SB 3, 9

high mountain | field | forest | sandy / rocky beach | wide river | deep lake | island | city | village | harbour | visit a castle | go hiking / climbing / mountain biking / (wind) surfing / pony trekking

Talk to a partner. Choose a place in the British Isles and take turns to talk about it.

6 How to describe places for a quiz → SB 3, 17

Ideas for tips:
- In this place you can …
- It's famous for …
- One of the attractions here is …
- If you want to …, you will … here.
- If you're interested in history, you should …
- It's in the north / east / south / west.
- … built it.

Make a quiz with a partner. Choose a place in the British Isles and give your partner tips about it. Can your partner guess the place? When your partner guesses right, then he/she gives tips for another place and you guess.

Talk about different kinds of texts

7 How to talk about stories and legends → SB 3, 24

Nouns: king | queen | wizard | hero / heroine | villain | knight | robber | outlaw
Adjectives: colourful | magical | brave | cruel | dangerous | powerful | mysterious
Phrases: to have a fight | to hide in the forest | to use your power | to solve a crime

Look at these pictures. The boys are playing the roles of three famous British legends. What do you think the stories are about? What do you know about them? Talk to a partner.

8 How to talk about poems → SB 3, 48

- The poem makes me feel …
- I'd describe the atmosphere as …
- The language in this poem is … while the other poem sounds …
- I think the poem is about …

You can use these phrases to talk about poems.

Useful phrases — Talk about different kinds of texts

9 How to express your opinion about news reports / articles → SB 3, 81

Phrases: I can't believe that people … | The article makes you think more about … | I hope more people will change … | Why do people …?

Adjectives: cruel | awful | sad | hopeful | …

You can use these phrases to tell how you feel about news reports and articles.

10 How to talk about fictional texts → SB 3, 108

- It feels like something scary / dangerous / … is happening. Words like … or … in line … tell me so.
- The lines … and … are both key lines because …

You can use these phrases to talk about parts of a fictional text.

11 How to talk about the main characters in a drama → SB 4, 31

- … tries to convince / persuade / tell / warn …
- The dilemma starts / problems start when …
- … seems / feels confused / unsure / convinced / angry / sad / …
- … has doubts about …
- I think Claire feels tempted …
- … tempts / teases …

You can use these phrases to talk about a scene from a drama.

12 How to talk about graphic novels → SB 4, 89

create suspense / a quiet atmosphere | make the reader live through / experience the story | show reactions / feelings of characters | introduce fast action / speed | create a distance

You can use these phrases to talk about the content and the effect graphic novels have on you.

13 How to talk about blog posts → SB 4, 102

You can't believe everything you read / see / … | With enough money / power, you can stage / fake / … | I bet a powerful company / the government / Hollywood could … | Something that big / complicated would be easy / impossible / … to fake.

You can use these phrases to express your opinion about the content of a blog post.

Talk about visuals

14 How to describe cartoons → SB 3, 44

"It helps him realise I'm being serious."

"Sorry, he's not here right now. He's in 14 other places."

In my opinion, the cartoon's message is … | I think the cartoon wants to show that … | The cartoonist wants us to think about … / wants to make fun of … | I agree / don't agree with the cartoon's message because …

You and your partner each choose one of the cartoons. Describe what you can see. What do you think the cartoon's message is? Do you agree with it? Explain why or why not.

15 How to talk about photos → SB 4, 40

- The picture on the left shows … while the picture on the right is an example of …
- The picture of … shows / represents / symbolizes …
- The picture is a way to say that people in America / Germany …

You can use these phrases to talk about and compare the scenery and situation in photos.

Useful phrases — How to argue and discuss

16 How to describe and analyze pictures → SB 4, 47

Describing pictures:
- In picture X, a person is talking / running / having fun with … / asking … | Somebody else is laughing / shouting / …
- In the foreground, there's a/an … / there's some …
- In the background, you see a/an … / lots of …

Analyzing pictures:
- In my opinion, the picture is a typical example of … because it shows …
- The picture represents … / shows …
- The picture tries to show … but I think a picture with … instead of … would work better because …

Work with a partner. Each of you chooses one of the photos. Take turns to describe your photo to your partner. First, describe what you can see and what is happening. Then analyze the picture and give your opinion about it.

17 How to write a film rating → SB 4, 105

well-developed / undeveloped / convincing characters | well-written / badly-written dialogue | a good performance / one of his / her very best performances | great / disappointing actors / acting | silly / weak / creative / believable / … plot | In my opinion … | If you ask me …

You and your partner each choose a film that you have recently seen. You each write a short rating (6–8 sentences) for it. Then read and edit each other's texts. Say if you like each other's rating and why.

How to argue and discuss

18 How to compromise → SB 3, 34

Why don't we …? | I don't think that's a good idea. | Yes, we should do that. | Can we meet halfway? | How do you feel about …? | I've got an idea. Can we …? | You've got a point but … | No, I don't mind doing that. | What do you think about …? | I don't think we can do that. | If we did it this way, we could … | It would be better to …

Role play: Choose one of the situations below and have a discussion with a partner. First decide which role each of you will play.

> You want a tattoo. Your mum / dad disagrees.

> Your best friend doesn't agree with the guest list for *your* birthday party.

> You have a great idea for a fun day with your family. But your brother / sister has other ideas.

> You have a new hobby. Your friend thinks it's a bad idea.

Useful phrases

19 How to persuade someone to change their behavior / express an attitude → SB 4, 69

Persuading someone to change their behavior
- You're going to get into so much trouble!
- You're so going to get detention!
- You'll be suspended if you …
- They have that rule because …
- I see your point but …
- You might be right but …
- You'd better … / You should … / Why don't you …?
- If I were you, I'd …

Expressing an attitude
- No risk, no fun!
- They want me to …
- They make me so mad!
- Why can't I …?
- They can't stop me …!
- I can't see the point of …
- It's a waste of time telling him / her …
- I don't understand why …

Role play: Your friend doesn't agree with a school rule and is about to break it. You don't want your friend to get into trouble so you try to persuade him/her not to break the rule. Choose from one of the situations below and write and act out the conversation.

fake hall pass so that he / she can skip classes

cheat in a test / use a cheat sheet

How to get along in everyday situations

20 How to talk about things to do in the country → SB 3, 114

Talk about which of these activities are interesting for you.

1. feeding animals
2. milking cows
3. exploring a cave
4. swimming in a lake
5. playing in an adventure playground
6. reading ghost stories
7. walking
8. geocaching

- I think … is dangerous / scary / exciting / boring / fantastic / a lot of fun / …
- I like farms, so … is the activity for me!
- … is fantastic / great / … for small children, but I like more interesting / more exciting / … activities like …
- I don't like sports, so I'm not into …

Useful phrases — How to get along in everyday situations

21 How to make dialogues at the travel agent's → SB 3, 16

Assistant:
- Hello, what can I do for you?
- How long would you like to stay?
- If you're into …, you'll …
- Do you want to go by car, by train or by coach? Do you need a ticket?
- Would you like to book a room / a flat / a house?
- If you want to …, you can …

Customer:
- I'd like to travel to … with …
- Over the weekend / two weeks / …
- We love … / We're into …
- How long does it take?
- We need … tickets.
- How much is it?
- Oh, I think that's too expensive.
- Yes, that's fine. Thank you.

Make a role play with a partner:
One of you is an assistant at a travel agent's. The other one is a customer who wants to go on holiday. Use the useful phrases to make dialogues.

22 How to keep the ball bouncing (doing small talk) → SB 3, 82

Hi. You're new here at / in …, right? | What do you think of …? | What's different about …? | Do you miss anything from …? | Are you enjoying …? | Have you ever …? | Why don't we …? | Have you tried …? | You should … | I've got a great tip: Check out the … I'm sure you'll like it. | Do you feel like hanging out? | If you have any questions / If there's anything you need, just let me know.
I'm … / My name is … | I feel (a bit) nervous / worried / excited / … | That's cool, cheers! | Can you tell me more about …? | I'd like to … | Do you have any favourite places to hang out? | What was that you mentioned about …? | Sorry, I didn't catch what you just said about …

With your partner, choose one of these situations.

> There's a new girl at school.
> A new boy has moved into the house next door.
> It's your first day at the sports club.

Now make small talk with the person in the situation you've chosen (your partner). You need a small ball. Every time you ask a question, bounce the ball to your partner. How long can you keep the ball bouncing?

23 How to break the ice → SB 4, 23

Icebreakers
I hope the train will arrive soon. | How long do you think we'll have to wait for …?! | How long have you been …? | I'm glad it isn't so crowded / busy / hot / cold here today. Yesterday it was so … | Cool T-shirt! You must be a … fan. | I've heard the film / show / band / … is really good. | Have you seen the latest film with …?

Role play: You're at a train station and your train is late. Another person is waiting for the train too. The person looks friendly and smiles at you. Together with a partner, write down a conversation you could have with him/her. Act out the conversation.

How to prepare and present different projects

24 How to tell a travel story → SB 4, 20

Did I tell you about …? | As I've already told you, … | … and then I realised / remembered that … | The next thing I knew … | A few seconds later … | The weirdest / funniest / scariest thing happened to me the other day. | After a while … | Anyway, it turned out that … | In the end, I decided to …

Talk to a partner. Use the phrases to tell each other an exciting travel story about your last holiday / trip. After you have told your stories, give each other feedback.

25 How to write a text for the yearbook → SB 4, 56

The swim / soccer / … team had their best season ever. | Being in / Participating in the Drama Club / the Yearbook Committee was … special / different / interesting this year because … | The Art Club started the year with … | Wasn't the Spring Dance / the championship basketball game the best ever? | We'll always remember the day when … | Here he / she is again with … | He / She will never learn! | We wanted you to see THIS! | How could we ever forget …?

*Student yearbooks are typically divided into the three main sections **Student Superlatives**, **Highlights of the Year** and **Clubs and Sports**. Work with a partner. Each of you chooses one of these three sections and writes a text for it. You can add funny pictures too if you want. Read each other's text and say what you like or don't like about it.*

Useful phrases — Talk about different topics

26 How to conduct a podcast interview → SB 4, 92

Small talk: This is a beautiful office / area / room. | How long have you been living / working here? | Where did you grow up?

Follow-up: Can you tell me more about …? | That's interesting. Tell me a little more about that. | But don't you think that …? | Can you explain that to me? | Sorry, I didn't catch that.

Getting specific: How long have you …? | How many …? | When did you …? | How often …? | How long had you been … (+-ing) before you became … / went … / found …

Open questions: What are your feelings about …? | What do you think about …? | What are your goals?

At the end: Thanks, I enjoyed talking to you. | Thank you very much for this interesting talk.

You can use these phrases when you write and record a podcast interview.

Talk about different topics

27 How to talk about different times in history → SB 3, 84

- I can imagine it was … when my grandparents were young because …
- Back then, people had / didn't have / could / couldn't …
- So it was easier / more difficult / cheaper / more expensive / nicer / … for them.
- I can't imagine how they … because they didn't have … like we do!

a) With a partner, talk about what you know about your grandparents' lives when they were your age. What was different to your life?

b) Now talk about what you think life was like a very long time ago, e.g. 500 or 1,000 years ago. For ideas, think of places in your town or region: castles, old walls, churches, …

28 How to talk about rules at your school → SB 4, 68

We can / can't | are / aren't allowed to | have to / don't have to …
… be late | eat / drink water | use our cell phones | shout | wear a uniform | be there without a teacher | skip classes | cheat | leave bags on the floor | …

If we break the rules / get caught …
- we have to stay after school | do extra work | stand outside | see the principal | …
- we are suspended | sent home
- we get detention
- our parents get a letter / phone call

With a partner, talk about rules at your school. Think of these situations:

corridor | cafeteria | gym | laboratory | classroom | computer room | library | outside

In the classroom

Tip

Die Wörter und Ausdrücke auf diesen Seiten musst du nicht auswendig lernen. Aber in vielen Situationen im Klassenzimmer wirst du sie nützlich finden!

Vocabulary for instructions and activities

(Die mit * gekennzeichneten Begriffe werden im Fachlehrplan von mindestens einem Bundesland als Operatoren definiert. Die Verwendung der geforderten Operatoren in Green Line beginnt in Band 1 und wird Band für Band ausgebaut.)

Act (out) one of the scenes. / Act (out) the dialogues.	Spiele eine der Szenen. / Spiele die Dialoge.
Add more words / ideas.	Füge weitere Wörter / Ideen hinzu.
Ask your partner questions.	Stelle deinem Partner / deiner Partnerin Fragen.
Answer your partner's questions.	Beantworte die Fragen deines Partners / deiner Partnerin.
Check your partner's text.	Überprüfe den Text deines Partners / deiner Partnerin.
Choose a character / one of the situations / options.	Wähle eine Figur / eine der Situationen / Optionen aus.
Collect ideas.	Sammle Ideen.
*Compare English and German.	Vergleiche das Englische und das Deutsche.
Complete the answers.	Vervollständige die Antworten.
Copy the grid / the mind map.	Schreibe die Tabelle / das Wörternetz ab.
Correct the wrong sentences.	Korrigiere die falschen Sätze.
*Describe what you see / how it makes you feel.	Beschreibe, was du siehst / wie du dich dabei fühlst.
Decide who writes which part.	Entscheidet, wer welchen Teil schreibt.
*Discuss different ideas.	Diskutiert verschiedene Ideen.
Divide your class up into two groups.	Teilt eure Klasse in zwei Gruppen auf.
Draw a picture.	Zeichne ein Bild.
Exchange your flyers / questions.	Tauscht eure Flyer / Fragen untereinander aus.
*Explain your answer. / Explain why.	Erkläre deine Antwort. / Erkläre warum.
Fill in your grid / the form.	Fülle deine Tabelle / das Formular aus.
Find the rule / the right word order.	Finde die Regel / die richtige Wortstellung.
Finish your brochure.	Stelle deine Broschüre fertig.
Form expert groups.	Bildet Expertengruppen.
Get organised.	Organisiert euch.
Give reasons / examples.	Nenne Gründe / Beispiele.
Give feedback.	Gib ein Feedback.
Go back to your home group.	Gehe zurück zu deiner ersten Gruppe.

A Anhang — In the classroom

Guess the new words.	Errate die neuen Wörter.
Imagine you're one of the people in the story.	Stelle dir vor, du bist eine der Personen in der Geschichte.
Improve your text / part of the report.	Verbessere deinen Text / deinen Teil des Berichts.
Learn your text by heart.	Lerne deinen Text auswendig.
Listen to the sentences / the dialogue.	Höre dir die Sätze / den Dialog an.
Look at the picture / the examples.	Schau dir das Bild / die Beispiele an.
***Look up** the words.	Schlage die Wörter nach.
Make a poster / a grid / a mind map / notes.	Fertige ein Poster / eine Tabelle / ein Wörternetz / Notizen an.
***Match** the sentence parts.	Ordne die Satzteile einander zu.
Note down what is missing.	Notiere, was fehlt.
Plan the scenes.	Plane die Szenen.
Practise your scenes / the dialogues.	Übe deine Szenen / die Dialoge.
***Present** the information from your text.	Präsentiere die Informationen aus deinem Text.
Put in the correct forms.	Setze die richtigen Formen ein.
Put the verbs in the right / correct form.	Bringe die Verben in die richtige Form.
Read your text aloud. / Read your text out loud.	Lies deinen Text laut vor.
Record your final report / dialogue.	Nehmt euren fertigen Bericht / Dialog auf.
Repeat the sentences / the dialogues.	Wiederhole die Sätze / die Dialoge.
***Report** what the people say.	Berichte, was die Leute sagen.
Say the words / the sounds.	Sage die Wörter / die Laute.
Scan the text for details.	Suche den Text nach Details ab.
Share the information with your partner.	Teile die Informationen mit deinem Partner / deiner Partnerin.
Skim the text for the gist.	Überfliege den Text und finde die wichtigsten Aussagen.
***Sum up / Summarise** what happens in the story.	Fasse zusammen, was in der Geschichte passiert.
Swap roles.	Tauscht die Rollen.
Take notes.	Mache dir Notizen.
Take turns.	Wechselt euch ab.
***Talk** with / to your partner (about …).	Sprich mit deinem Partner / deiner Partnerin (über …).
***Tell** your partner about your experiences.	Erzähle deinem Partner / deiner Partnerin von deinen Erfahrungen.
Think about different problems.	Denke über verschiedene Probleme nach.
Think of ideas for …	Überlege dir Ideen für …
***Translate** the words / sentences.	Übersetze die Wörter / Sätze.
Underline the words that change.	Unterstreiche die Wörter, die sich ändern.
Use the ideas / the vocabulary.	Verwende die Ideen / die Vokabeln.
Watch the film.	Sieh dir den Film an.
Work with a partner or in a group.	Arbeite mit einem Partner / einer Partnerin oder in einer Gruppe.
***Write** dialogues / a short text / a reply / a summary.	Schreibe Dialoge / einen kurzen Text / eine Antwort / eine Zusammenfassung.
Write about your friends.	Schreibe über deine Freunde.
Write down your ideas / key words.	Schreibe deine Ideen / Schlüsselwörter auf.

Irregular verbs

- ■ ■ ■ Grundform, *simple past* und *past participle* sind identisch
- ■ ● ● Grundform unterscheidet sich vom *simple past* und *past participle*
- ■ ● ■ Grundform und *past participle* sind identisch, nur das *simple past* hat eine andere Form
- ■ ● ▲ Grundform, *simple past* und *past participle* haben alle eine andere Form

■ Grundform	■ simple past	■ past participle	Deutsch
cost [kɒst]	cost [kɒst]	cost [kɒst]	kosten
cut [kʌt]	cut [kʌt]	cut [kʌt]	schneiden
hit [hɪt]	hit [hɪt]	hit [hɪt]	schlagen, treffen
hurt [hɜ:t]	hurt [hɜ:t]	hurt [hɜ:t]	verletzen, sich weh tun
let [let]	let [let]	let [let]	lassen
put [pʊt]	put [pʊt]	put [pʊt]	legen, setzen, stellen
set up ['set ˌʌp]	set up ['set ˌʌp]	set up ['set ˌʌp]	erbauen, errichten
upset [ʌp'set]	upset [ʌp'set]	upset [ʌp'set]	aus der Fassung bringen

■ Grundform	● simple past	● past participle	Deutsch
bring [brɪŋ]	brought [brɔ:t]	brought [brɔ:t]	(mit)bringen
build [bɪld]	built [bɪlt]	built [bɪlt]	bauen
burn [bɜ:n]	burnt [bɜ:nt]	burnt [bɜ:nt]	(ver)brennen
buy [baɪ]	bought [bɔ:t]	bought [bɔ:t]	kaufen
catch [kætʃ]	caught [kɔ:t]	caught [kɔ:t]	fangen; mitbekommen
dream [dri:m]	dreamed [dri:md] / dreamt [dremt]	dreamed [dri:md] / dreamt [dremt]	träumen
feel [fi:l]	felt [felt]	felt [felt]	fühlen
find [faɪnd]	found [faʊnd]	found [faʊnd]	finden
get [get]	got [gɒt]	got [gɒt]	bekommen; werden
hang [hæŋ]	hung [hʌŋ]	hung [hʌŋ]	hängen
have [hæv]	had [hæd]	had [hæd]	haben
hear [hɪə]	heard [hɜ:d]	heard [hɜ:d]	hören
hold [həʊld]	held [held]	held [held]	halten
keep [ki:p]	kept [kept]	kept [kept]	(auf)bewahren, behalten
lead [li:d]	led [led]	led [led]	(an)führen
learn [lɜ:n]	learned [lɜ:nd] / learnt [lɜ:nt]	learned [lɜ:nd] / learnt [lɜ:nt]	lernen
leave [li:v]	left [left]	left [left]	(ver)lassen
lend [lend]	lent [lent]	lent [lent]	(ver)leihen
make [meɪk]	made [meɪd]	made [meɪd]	machen, tun
meet [mi:t]	met [met]	met [met]	treffen
pay [peɪ]	paid [peɪd]	paid [peɪd]	(be)zahlen
read [ri:d]	read [red]	read [red]	lesen
say [seɪ]	said [sed]	said [sed]	sagen
sell [sel]	sold [səʊld]	sold [səʊld]	verkaufen
send [send]	sent [sent]	sent [sent]	senden, verschicken
shoot [ʃu:t]	shot [ʃɒt]	shot [ʃɒt]	schießen (auf)
sit [sɪt]	sat [sæt]	sat [sæt]	sitzen
sleep [sli:p]	slept [slept]	slept [slept]	schlafen

smell [smel]	smelt [smelt]	smelt [smelt]	riechen, duften
spell [spel]	spelt [spelt]	spelt [spelt]	buchstabieren
spend [spend]	spent [spent]	spent [spent]	ausgeben, verbringen
spill [spɪl]	spilt [spɪlt]	spilt [spɪlt]	verschütten, auslaufen
stand (up) [stænd]	stood (up) [stʊd]	stood (up) [stʊd]	(auf)stehen
sting [stɪŋ]	stung [stʌŋ]	stung [stʌŋ]	stechen
teach [tiːtʃ]	taught [tɔːt]	taught [tɔːt]	lehren, unterrichten
tell [tel]	told [təʊld]	told [təʊld]	erzählen
think [θɪŋk]	thought [θɔːt]	thought [θɔːt]	(nach)denken, glauben
understand [ˌʌndəˈstænd]	understood [ˌʌndəˈstʊd]	understood [ˌʌndəˈstʊd]	verstehen
win [wɪn]	won [wʌn]	won [wʌn]	gewinnen, siegen

■ Grundform	● simple past	■ past participle	Deutsch
become [bɪˈkʌm]	became [bɪˈkeɪm]	become [bɪˈkʌm]	werden
come [kʌm]	came [keɪm]	come [kʌm]	kommen
run [rʌn]	ran [ræn]	run [rʌn]	laufen, rennen

■ Grundform	● simple past	▲ past participle	Deutsch
be [biː]	was / were [wɒz / wɜː]	been [biːn]	sein
blow (out) [bləʊ]	blew [bluː]	blown [bləʊn]	(aus)blasen, (aus)pusten
break [breɪk]	broke [brəʊk]	broken [ˈbrəʊkn]	(zer)brechen, kaputt machen
choose [tʃuːz]	chose [tʃəʊz]	chosen [tʃəʊzn]	(aus)wählen
do [duː]	did [dɪd]	done [dʌn]	machen, tun
draw [drɔː]	drew [druː]	drawn [drɔːn]	zeichnen
drink [drɪŋk]	drank [dræŋk]	drunk [drʌŋk]	trinken
drive [draɪv]	drove [drəʊv]	driven [ˈdrɪvn]	fahren
eat [iːt]	ate [et]	eaten [iːtn]	essen
fall [fɔːl]	fell [fel]	fallen [ˈfɔːlən]	fallen
fly [flaɪ]	flew [fluː]	flown [fləʊn]	fliegen
forget [fəˈget]	forgot [fəˈgɒt]	forgotten [fəˈgɒtn]	vergessen
give [gɪv]	gave [geɪv]	given [ˈgɪvn]	geben
go [gəʊ]	went [went]	gone [gɒn]	gehen, fahren
grow [grəʊ]	grew [gruː]	grown [grəʊn]	wachsen; anbauen
know [nəʊ]	knew [njuː]	known [nəʊn]	kennen, wissen
ring [rɪŋ]	rang [ræŋ]	rung [rʌŋ]	klingeln; anrufen
rise [raɪz]	rose [rəʊz]	risen [ˈrɪzn]	steigen, sich erheben
see [siː]	saw [sɔː]	seen [siːn]	sehen
show [ʃəʊ]	showed [ʃəʊd]	shown [ʃəʊn]	zeigen
sing [sɪŋ]	sang [sæŋ]	sung [sʌŋ]	singen
sink [sɪŋk]	sank [sæŋk]	sunk [sʌŋk]	sinken, untergehen
speak [spiːk]	spoke [spəʊk]	spoken [ˈspəʊkn]	sprechen
swim [swɪm]	swam [swæm]	swum [swʌm]	schwimmen
take [teɪk]	took [tʊk]	taken [ˈteɪkn]	nehmen
throw [θrəʊ]	threw [θruː]	thrown [θrəʊn]	werfen
wake up [ˌweɪkˈʌp]	woke up [ˌwəʊkˈʌp]	woken up [ˌwəʊknˈʌp]	aufwachen; aufwecken
wear [weə]	wore [wɔː]	worn [wɔːn]	anhaben, tragen
write [raɪt]	wrote [rəʊt]	written [ˈrɪtn]	schreiben